MAKING ME
HAPPEN
WORKBOOK

*A fun and interactive guide to help tweens/teens unearth
and promote their best selves*

TAAYOO A MURRAY

MAKING ME
HAPPEN

Making Me Happen by Taayoo A Murray

© 2017 by Taayoo A Murray. All rights reserved.

Books may be purchased by contacting the publisher and author at:

Cover Design: Cover Design Studio

Interior Design: Tackees Bruen

Publisher: Higher Heights Press

Editor: Global English Editing

Eduting: Katie Smyth

ISBN: 978-0-692-86671-9

Self Help

First Edition

Printed in USA

For my parents, Glen and Rowena Murray. Thanks for Making Me Happen.

ACKNOWLEDGEMENTS

**No one who achieves success does so without the help of others.
The wise and confident acknowledge this help with gratitude."**

- Alfred North Whitehead

I have the opportunity of being surrounded by the most supportive people anyone could ask for. There are some I would like to express my heartfelt thanks to. Firstly, I would like publicly acknowledge my Lord and Savior Jesus Christ, whom I give all the credit for inspiring this book and orchestrating the circumstances for it to come to fruition. I would also like to give a big shout out to my graphic designer, Tackees Bruen, who was able to take my ideas and make them into visionary excellence. Thanks also to my publicist, Angelle of JKS Communications. You gave my work presence and made the experience even more exciting, thanks a million! To my family, thanks for giving me true confidence in self, and complete assurance that you would ALWAYS be there. Lastly and by no means least, to Marlon, Mikhail and Kyle-Patric Eaton. You men are truly the best part of me. Your unwavering love and support has never gone unnoticed or unappreciated.

I love you guys endlessly!

To everyone else who assisted in any way, no matter how small, thanks for your input!

TABLE
OF CONTENTS

WHAT TO EXPECT
- *An introduction to the personal SWOT analysis*
- *How to maximize your strengths and manage around your weaknesses*
- *Learn how to document and develop the image that you want*

WHAT TO EXPECT
- *How to define action goals vs results goals*
- *Learn how to set SMAC-able goals*
- *Learn how to develop a weekly plan*

WHAT TO EXPECT
- *Learn the importance of time management*
- *Learn how to use the time quadrant to manage daily tasks*
- *How to master controllables to mitigate against uncontrollables*

INTRODUCTION

All glory comes from daring to begin.
– Eugene F. Ware

Welcome! The starting point of all achievement is desire. Deciding to even read this book demonstrates your desire to make a positive change in your life, and for that I give you a standing ovation! The beginning is always the toughest. That's when you have to try to dim all the voices crowding your space, shouting all their opinions at you. The loudest voice of all is your own self-doubt and fear. It tries to lure you back into a false sense of safety, frightening you with the fear of the unknown.

Go ahead, look that fear in the face, sneer at him and say **stand back**! You are tired of mediocrity! There is more to you and you're going to unearth it!

Your environs are now quiet, the voices are silent, **you** made them mute. The stage is set, it's time to **Make Me Happen.**

HOW TO USE THIS BOOK

This book is meant to be used an interactive tool that will result in the development of life changing habits. All activities are meant to be completed. Take as much time as needed, focusing on the process not the result. Remember real change takes time ☺.

Navigation Icons

- *Indicator for brainstorming questions*

- *Indicator for tips*

- *Indicator for writing exercises*

1
SECTION

ME,
MYSELF AND I

Change is hard at first, messy in the middle and gorgeous at the end.

– Robin Sharma

WHAT TO EXPECT

• An introduction to the personal SWOT analysis

• How to maximize your strengths and manage around your weaknesses

• Learn how to document and develop the image that you want

"What is the definition of definition?" asked my 12-year-old once. *Definition* means the act of defining, or of making something definite, distinct or clear. Unfortunately, many of us allow other persons, circumstances, or even events/episodes in our lives to define us. Notwithstanding the value of another's opinion or advice, is it worth more than our own with regard to ourselves? This opens up another can of worms. Sadly, many of us see ourselves in a worse light than how others view us. Whether we see actually a true reflection of reality when we look into that all too honest mirror, mirror on the wall is indeed debatable. However, let's pretend for a second that what we see is indeed the worst picture. Whether it's the freckled face, fat thighs *(note to self ☹)* or something more intrinsic like a character flaw, there is good news! You can change it! Don't take my word for it, check out some authentic sources. For Christians like myself, the Bible in Isaiah 1:18 says, *"Come now, let us settle the matter,"* says the Lord, *"though your sins are like scarlet, they shall be as white as snow; though they are red as crimson, they shall be like wool."*

The secular among us may not accept this readily, so let us look at some real-world examples. According to the *Business Insider* article, *The 10 Most Successful Rebranding Campaigns Ever,* (by Judith Aquino, February 2011), Burberry was once considered gang wear, and now it's worn by Emma Watson and Kate Moss. Due to rumors that the Burberry was popular amongst hooligans, two pubs in Leicester famously banned anyone wearing the label. New leadership and savvy product design are what transformed the brand into one of the hottest fashion labels.

The second makeover is McDonald's. McDonald's was thought to make America fat. Now it looks like Starbucks and serves salads. McDonald's had been increasingly worn down by the image of being a low-brow and un-healthy restaurant chain. It has since tried to rebrand itself as more health conscious with a greater variety of salads and other healthy meal options.

Lastly, Apple was nearly bankrupt; now it's ruling the world. In 1997, Apple was veering dangerously close to bankruptcy. Nearly 19 years later, stock prices have skyrocketed and the company is stronger than ever. Therefore, it is safe to say rebranding can be done. God says so, and McDonald's and Apple have done it. Compared to them you are a petty project! However, will it be easy? Will it happen overnight? No, of course not, but it is possible. Rebranding requires more than just changing appearances. It demands creating a vision that inspires others to see you in a new light.

> *"Rebranding requires more than just changing appearances. It demands creating a vision that inspires others to see you in a new light."*

Now that we know it's possible, how do we do it? I am a sucker for the 1–2–3 process, simplify, simplify, simplify. Let us backtrack a bit. How did you create your current brand? The operative phrase being '**you** create.' Yes, you're the one who created the brand you currently have, subcon-sciously or not, through your choice of dress, hairstyle, jewelry, friends, hang-out spots, music, speech . . . the list goes on. I know, I know, all my liberals are up in arms right now saying you have no right to judge me by the way I look. Guess what? I do have the right. When you see someone for the first time, without speaking or interacting with them, you form impressions. What allows you to form that impression? Yes, my dears, the way they look. You know nothing about them, so their look is all you have to go on. And before you get all self-righteous on me, we have all seen that hot guy or girl, and have started drooling. Then we find out something about their character that turns us off. Unfortunately, we didn't **see** their character and we were drooling at the eye candy.

Now back to rebranding. Before we throw out the baby with the bath water, let's take stock of ourselves. After all, there must be something good to salvage. We call this doing our personal SWOT analysis. We're going to look at our strengths, our weaknesses, opportunities and threats. The aim is to fully utilize our strengths, understand our weaknesses so that we can manage around them, identify opportunities for growth, and recognize threats to our development so that we can lessen their effects.

Please see table below.

Now remember, true rebranding has to happen internally **and** externally because we are launching the whole product. Don't be afraid, make your lists internal and external, be honest and be detailed. For example:

SWOT ANALYSIS TABLE

FIGURE 1

INTERNAL FACTORS	
STRENGTHS (+)	**WEAKNESSES (-)**
Talk about what you're good at, your unique assets and resources, and how your positive attributes are perceived by others.	*Talk about improvements you need to make, any resources you lack, and how these negative attributes might be perceived by others.*
EXTERNAL FACTORS	
OPPORTUNITIES (+)	**THREATS (-)**
List doors that are currently open to you, opportunities you can capitalize on, and how your strenghts can create new connections.	*List any harmful hazards, competitors, and how known weaknesses can open the door to threats.*

FIGURE 1. *Example of a SWOT Analysis.*

FIGURE 1.1

INTERNAL FACTORS	
STRENGTHS (+)	**WEAKNESSES (-)**
Good writing skills	*Procrastination*
EXTERNAL FACTORS	
OPPORTUNITIES (+)	**THREATS (-)**
Public speaking classes	*Fear of failure*

FIGURE 1.1 *Example of how SWOT Analysis should be filled out.*

In writing this book, I have come to one very important conclusion. I now know my greatest strengths, what I excel at, and I will use those skill sets to chart my path to ultimate success and fulfillment. Crafting your personal SWOT analysis is a great way to begin the journey of identifying your strengths. But what is a strength? My favorite definition comes from the book *Now, Discover Your Strengths,* by Buckingham & Clifton. They say a strength is "consistent near-perfect performance in an activity."

What do you do that comes naturally with almost no effort, and is perfectly executed at all times?

Following this logic, What do you do that comes naturally with almost no effort, and is perfectly executed at all times? We all know our strengths, but have been more conditioned to focus on improving our weaknesses, much to our peril. My aim is for you to identify and hone your God-given talents, allowing them to either overshadow or compensate for your weaknesses. I highly recommend the Gallup's *Strength Finder* profile to learn more about your top five strengths.

Having refocused your attention on what you naturally excel at, aka your strengths, you need to take some deliberate steps to ensure that those pesky weaknesses do not sabotage you on your path to success. Once again, I believe in simplify, simplify, simplify.

G E T H E L P ! On your journey to make yourself happen, you will need help. That person will be your accountability partner. Ideally, your accountability partner will help hold you accountable for preset goals. However, you can enlist the help of someone else in your quest for greatness. For example, I am not very good with details and can easily forget things. So as crazy as it sounds, in addition to writing lists and setting alarms/reminders, I ask different people to remind me about specific tasks. The results is that my weakness of memory is supported by other helpful persons.

SMOTHER WEAKNESS WITH STRENGTH

While this may not always work, it is definitely worth a try. Let's discuss the game of soccer. The role of the attacking forward is to be very fast and create opportunities for scoring. Forwards are naturally offensive players. The defensive player's role is to ensure that the as much as possible the ball stays in the opponent's half and doesn't get near his goal. Both players are extremely skillful in their area, but it is very rare to find one player that plays both positions equally well. The point being, no one cares that the forward is a poor defender as long as he keeps on scoring. And no one cares that the defender can't shoot, as long as he protects the goal.

"When you're consistently performing perfectly in one area, people tend to forget about what you're not good at."

W O R K Sometimes avoiding your weakness is not possi-
AT IT ! ble. So if you're the student council representa-
tive, you may have excellent leadership skills and the ability to
inspire persons. You may, however, suck at organizing and han-
dling details. While poor organizing skills by itself may not cause
you to fail in your role, it can certainly undermine your efforts
for success. In this case it may be advisable that you try to improve those skill sets, thus heightening your chances of success.

F O R G E T In some cases, the area that you are weak-
A B O U T I T ! est in may not matter in the least bit. For
example, we live in a world where being sociable is hip. Therefore, you get caught up in constantly staying in touch with everyone, updating social media and always putting yourself out
there. Guess what? You don't have to. Being polite and having
the ability to take part in a meaningful conversation is in no way
synonymous with constant chatter and internet presence. The
latter doesn't make you more personable. Being labeled an in-
trovert isn't a bad thing, and there are other ways to make your
mark other than Snapchat.

One of our biggest enemies to self-improvement is fear of failure. We're
so afraid to fail that we don't even try. Let me clue you in on something:
If you're considering a rebranding project, then what you're working with
isn't so hot, so what do you have to lose?

Now that you have identified your strengths, and decided how to manage
around your weaknesses, we can begin.

STEP
01
DECIDE HOW YOU WANT TO BE SEEN

How do you want to be seen? This is totally up to you. Develop a mental picture of how you want to be seen by persons. Remember that physical attributes can be modified (although the scale of change is limited) to create the persona you want to project. What this means is that while the average female will say she wants to look like Beyoncé, upon deep reflection it's not actually the physical image that she wants to replicate, but what Beyoncé's persona communicates – confidence, power, sex appeal, success. None of these attributes are synonymous with a particular body type.

How do you want to be seen?

_____

_____

_____

_____

_____

_____

_____

_____

STEP
02
DOCUMENT YOUR IMAGE

"A plan that is not documented is a mere idea and has an more than 95% chance of not coming to fruition."

This is now your blueprint, or plan. A plan that is not documented is a mere idea and has an more than 95% chance of not coming to fruition. Be detailed in your plan about how you want to be seen. Focus more on the impressions you want to leave with persons instead of physical attributes, as these can be created. For example, *I want people to see me as an attractive, confident woman who can achieve anything. Or, I want to be seen as a strong, brave and good-looking guy who can relate to everyone.* This is a stark difference to *I want to be pretty or handsome.* This is so important because beauty is in the eye of the beholder, and our aim is to **create** what we want people to behold.

_____

_____

_____

_____

STEP
03
DEVELOP AN ACTION PLAN FOR REBRANDING PROJECT AND BE REALISTIC

(see appendix for template)

Depending on the image you're trying to create, this may take months. It takes on average 21 days of consistent behavior to learn a habit, but once learnt it is extremely hard to break. I can share a personal story with you: I had decided that I wanted to develop the habit of showering every night before going to bed. Sounds simple, but that's just me. I consistently did it for a month. To this day I cannot sleep without showering. No matter how tired I am, even if I fall asleep, I wake up in the middle of the night to shower.

"It takes on average 21 days of consistent behavior to learn a habit."

(Private coaching is available, go to www.taayoomurray.com to schedule a free consultation.)

_____

_____

_____

_____

_____

_____

_____

_____

_____

_____

STEP
04
REWARD YOURSELF

How do you plan to reward yourself and when?

Rebranding is hard and sometimes discouraging work. People in general hate change, so your efforts will not be welcome. Remember, however, that you're changing in essence a culture, so resistance is inevitable. Treat yourself when you hit your major milestones but don't forget to celebrate the private victories. If gaining confidence is part of the rebranding project, reward yourself on progress. You know where you started, and rewarding yourself for the incremental successes will go a long way towards achieving your ultimate goal. And just like any other plan, document it. How do you plan to reward yourself and when? Having something to look forward will make the journey that much more bearable.

Summary

Things to do after completing this section:

- Develop your personal SWOT analysis, focusing on your strengths.

- Decide how you want to be seen and document it.

- Document your action plan to achieve this goal.

- Remember to reward yourself and BREATHE!

NOTES

SECTION

2

THE
EXTRA MILE

Do more than is required. What is the distance between someone who achieves their goals consistently and those who spend their lives and careers merely following? The extra mile.

– Gary Ryan Blair

WHAT TO EXPECT

- How to define action goals vs results goals
- Learn how to set SMAC-able goals
- Learn how to develop a weekly plan

> **"What we don't realize is that nothing happens accidentally. Huge successes are planned, and so are huge failures."**

How many times have you heard the saying, "if you fail to plan, plan to fail?" Truer words have never been spoken! What we don't realize is that nothing happens accidentally. Huge successes are planned, and so are huge failures. People who enjoy success consistently work towards it and people who fail consistently also consistently work towards failure. You may ask, how does someone consistently work towards failure? By consistently not taking an active part in their life choices and just continuously meandering through life. Wasting their life became their plan, and failure is the result.

> **How does someone consistently work towards failure?**

Now I don't want anyone to become overwhelmed because they don't have some master plan for their life typed and saved somewhere, and are meticulously checking off the boxes as you move along. This is the biggest set up for failure! Remember, I am the queen of easy does it, so once again simplify, simplify, simplify.

It would be nice if you could get up today and create a one-year plan and execute it, but Rome wasn't built in a day. I have a friend who every year develops a list of things that she wants to do or accomplish that year, and she ticks them off as she goes along. That same friend has her monthly budget written down and in her purse and can pull it out whenever (shout out to Short Stuff ☺). Not all of us have those innate characteristics, but goal-setting and execution is integral to any kind of success.

Firstly, let's define what goals are. A goal is the intention of an activity or a plan. Therefore, it's a point of reference. Imagine leaving the house to go to the mall. You know which mall you're going to and how to get there. Every turn you take is influenced by making sure you get to the mall. The hilarious thing about most of us is that in our lives, we all have an idea of which "mall" we want to get to but never end up getting there. It's a combination of two things. We either know how to get there and sometimes get on the wrong bus (some of us miss our stop ☺), or take a wrong turn. Or some of us know which "mall" we want to get to, but literally don't know the directions and can't be bothered to get a GPS or ask for directions.

> *"A goal is the intention of an activity or a plan."*

Fear, of course, is another great immobilizer. We're afraid to get lost on our way there, or God forbid something should happen to us on the way. So the easiest thing to do is to stay home and watch the commercials of what is on sale at the "mall"! But what is fear? Fear is defined as 'a distressing emotion aroused by impending danger, whether real or imagined'. The Bible in Mark 5:36 says, Jesus told him: "Don't be afraid; just believe." Sounds simple right? However, some of us don't even have the faith of a mustard seed and need some support or crutches to move. That's what your goals and plans are for.

TIPS
TO MAKE GOAL-SETTING SUCCESSFUL

LOOK IN SO YOU CAN LOOK OUT

Introspection is a tough job. It's hard because it forces us to examine our intimate places, consider things

"Am I satisfied with where I am and what I have accomplished?"

we don't want to see. Truly looking in is an evaluation process. Take a scan of your life. Write down where you currently are and what you have accomplished. Then ask the big question: "Am I satisfied with where I am and what I have accomplished?"

This now becomes your ground zero, your baseline.

Go ahead, make your list!

_____

_____

_____

_____

_____

_____

_____

_____

_____

_____

_____

_____

_____

_____

SAY WHAT YOU WANT

Too often we have been conditioned to believe that wanting more is selfish, almost as if we don't have the right to want more than we currently have. My mission is to prove the naysayers wrong. Every dream is your right if you are willing to work to achieve it. So go ahead, think about what you want, what excites and thrills you. Most importantly, document it. A documented dream or plan has a greater than 95% chance of coming to fruition than an undocumented one.

What do **you** want? Go ahead, write it down!

_____

_____

_____

_____

_____

_____

_____

_____

_____

_____

_____

_____

_____

HAVE S-M-A-C- ABLE GOALS

Specific:

Make your goals specific. Be detailed in outlining them. For example, don't just say you want a car. Say you want a blue Nissan Maxima sedan.

Measurable:

Your goals should be quantitative and time-bound. This makes it possible to easily ascertain when you hit your goals. For example, "I will achieve 85% in four subjects by the end of the semester."

Attainable:

Make sure there exists the possibility for your dreams to come to fruition. Don't set targets for things that are not physically possible or exist outside of the borders of reality.

Challenging:

Our goals should always be something that we strive for. Having said this, they should require some effort on our part to achieve them. If our goals do not require that we flex our muscles, then they are not challenging

and need to be reviewed. The very concept of a dream or goal is that it is something that inspires us to move outside of ourselves in effort. This defines a real challenge.

FIND AN ACCOUNTABILITY PARTNER

It would be lovely if we could set goals and can achieve without any external help. Unfortunately, many preset goals die a natural death. The main reason for this is not having someone to pester us until we hit our targets. This individual is our accountability partner. When we say that we're going to complete that 2000-word essay by Friday, our accountability partner is the person who calls us every day to make sure that we start writing.

Now remember when I spoke about keeping things simple? Let's do just that. Let us start by setting a goal for tomorrow and making a plan to achieve it. Let's say my goal is to get to school/work on time tomorrow (I know this may seem to be a monumental goal for some of us ☺).

STEP
01
SET YOUR GOAL – I WILL ARRIVE AT SCHOOL/WORK AT 8.20AM

Now remember your goals are always written in the future tense, and must be S-M-A-C-able. That is, they must be specific, measurable, attainable and yet challenging. For example, saying I will get to school early tomorrow is not S-M-A-C-able. What time is early? Step 1 is defined as your result goals. This clearly states what you want the outcome of your actions to be.

"Your goals are always written in the future tense, and must be S-M-A-C-able. That is, they must be specific, measurable, attainable and yet challenging."

"Your result goals clearly states what you want the outcome of your actions to be."

STEP
02
DEVELOP YOUR PLAN OF ACTION GOALS.

List the actions that you will take to be able to get to school/work at 8.20am. This may include having your bag packed and clothes selected from the night before. It may include setting the alarm for a certain time. It may mean checking the bus or train schedule the night before to see if there are any planned changes. All of these are called action goals. Action goals are your GPS to getting to where you want to go.

"Action goals are your GPS to getting to where you want to go."

RESULT GOAL	ACTION GOAL
I will get to school at 8.20am every morning	Set my alarm for 7am

STEP
03
EXECUTE

You know what you want to do and how to get it done, so what's left? Just do it!

"Don't focus on the results, perfect the process and the results will come."

See how simple that was? In a nutshell it is these same steps that you take to get you to the top of your Mount Everest. But you'll never get there if you can't tackle your tomorrow. Focus on the little things, develop small good habits, and over time these small habits will become the new you. Don't focus on the results, perfect the process and the results will come. It is an organic process.

I recommend setting aside 30 minutes every Sunday to plan your week. Think about what you want to achieve each week. Remember simplify, simplify, simplify. It could be something simple as being early every day, or staying awake for the entire History class ☺. The important thing is the becoming and developing the habit of planning what happens in your life every day, instead of allowing circumstances to dictate your life. You may not always hit all your targets. The important thing is to evaluate, adjust, and keep pressing forward.

I have included a weekly plan template (see appendices) for you to use when making your plan. It embodies the total you – mind, body and soul – so that you can practice making holistic plans.

Summary

Things to do after completing this section:

- Develop a weekly plan.

NOTES

SECTION

3

THE 2T's:
TIME AND TAKING CONTROL

Prioritizing is an important aspect of productivity. Listed tasks should be things that matter: things that are in alignment with your objectives and do not distract you from what you really should be doing.

– Romuald Andrade

WHAT TO EXPECT

- Learn the importance of time management
- Learn how to use the time quadrant to manage daily tasks
- How to master controllables to mitigate against uncontrollables

We complain every day that we don't have enough time. We need more time to sleep, more time for vacation, more television time . . . the list goes on. However, time is one of the few constants in life. Contrary to what people may think, we all get the same amount of time each day. The only difference is how we use it. Ironically, the people with the most to do tend to accomplish more than the ones that have so little to do. The trick? Aha! It's that pesky little sucker called time management. Now I used to hate the term before, because whenever I heard the term time management I would immediately become defensive, thinking I was being accused of being disorganized and procrastinating (of course it was true ☺). However, time management tools are not just for the high-powered executives. They are also useful to the lazy among us who just want to get the boring stuff out of the way, so that we can move on to the fun things that we want to do.

WHAT IS TIME MANAGEMENT?

Time management is the coordination of tasks and activities to maximize the effectiveness of an individual's efforts. Essentially, the purpose of time management is enabling people to get more and better work done in less time. Time management is marketed as the tool of the super-efficient, industrious world. The truth is that they have discovered the secret to being able to do what they really want – organizing their time to leave space for their pleasures.

"Time management is the coordination of tasks and activities to maximize the effectiveness of an individual's efforts."

THE IMPORTANCE OF TIME MANAGEMENT

Reduces stress

One of the greatest stress inducers is the inability to get everything done in the allotted time. The constant worry of missed deadlines, and the perception ofinefficiency and inadequacy, can develop into anything from chronic migraines to stomach ulcers.

Once you learn how to manage your time, you no longer subject yourself to that level of stress. You're better able to estimate how long a given task will take you to complete, and you know you can meet the deadline.

Time is Limited

No matter how you slice it, there are only 24 hours in a day. The same goes for the President, the school principal, the store clerk, and you and I. By managing your time efficiently, you can accomplish more with less effort. Effective time management results in a more focused existence, as you will have clearly outlined what you plan to do, when you're going to do it, and how you're going to get it done. Tasks will then become less cumbersome as you would have prioritized them and devised ways of executing them that produce the best results with minimum effort.

"Effective time management results in a more focused existence"

Improved decision-making ability

One of the worries of insufficient time is feeling pressured into acting on the fly. Taking hurried decisions not only has the potential to be detrimental, it is the breeding ground of inefficiency, as the most prudent decisions are rarely taken in haste.

Through effective time management, you can eliminate the pressure that comes from feeling like you don't have enough time. You'll start to feel more calm and in control. When the time comes to examine options and decide, instead of rushing through the process, you can take time to carefully consider each option. And when you're able to do that, you diminish your chances of making a bad decision.

Become a more successful person

Mastering time management is integral in attaining success. It allows you to take control of your life rather than following the flow of others. As you accomplish more each day, make more sound decisions, and feel more in control, people notice. Ultimately, effective time management skills allow you to decide what **really** needs to get done and then **do** it. Executing key tasks and achieving your goals is the definition of a successful person.

"Executing key tasks and achieving your goals is the definition of a successful person."

'Me' time is necessary

A friend of mine once dated a guy who couldn't find time to fit everything in, including her. One weekend when she asked him why there was no time for her, he responded: "Honey, after I finish all my work, I have to spend time with me." As girlfriends, we were furious, but we have since come to acknowledge the wisdom of his words.

Everyone needs time to relax and unwind. Unfortunately, though, many of us don't get enough of it. Between school, jobs, family responsibilities, and errands, most of us are hard-pressed to find even 10 minutes to sit and do nothing.

Having good time management skills helps you find that time. When you're busy, you're getting more done. You accumulate extra time throughout your day that you can use later to relax, unwind, and prepare for a good night's sleep, or get your social media fix ☺.

Self-discipline is valuable

When you practice good time management, you leave no room for procrastination. The better you get at it, the more self-discipline you learn. This is a valuable skill that will begin to impact other areas of your life where a lack of discipline has kept you from achieving a goal.

STEP
01
MAKE A LIST OF EVERYTHING YOU MUST GET DONE

And I mean everything: From the science project to the face time with "bae". Examples: buy pens for class, check price for new shoes, and submit math homework, etc. The list is done when you cannot think of anything else that you need to do.

Stephen Covey developed a brilliant tool to help us manage and optimize our use of time. This tool is called the time quadrant (see diagram below). The quadrant, as the name suggests, has four sections named as follows:

Quadrant 1: Urgent & Important – contains tasks and responsibilities that need immediate attention.

Quadrant 2: Important & Not Urgent – contains items that are important without requiring immediate attention.

Quadrant 3: Urgent & Not important – contains items that are urgent without being important, often considered distractions.

Quadrant 4: Not Urgent & Not Important – focuses on tasks that do not yield any value.

TIME QUADRANT TABLE
FIGURE 2

	NOT URGENT	URGENT
IMPORTANT	**1. THE PROCRASTINATOR** • Exam tomorrow • Friend gets injured • Late for work • Project due today • Car breaks down	**2. THE PRIORITIZER** • Planning, Goal setting • Essay due in a week • Exercise • Relationships • Relaxation
NOT IMPORTANT	**3. THE YES - MAN** • Unimportant phone calls • Interruptions • Other peoples' small problems • Peer pressure	**4. THE SLACKER** • Too much TV • Endless phone calls/ texting/facebook • Excessive computer games • Mall Marathons • Time wasters

FIGURE 2. *Example of a Time Quadrant. Adapted from The 7 Habits of Highly Effective Teens by Stephen Covey.*

STEP
02
PLACE ALL ITEMS ON THE TO-DO LIST IN THE APPROPRIATE BOX IN THE TIME QUADRANT

Aha! All of a sudden the list becomes manageable because it becomes glaringly obvious what our priorities should be and where our energies should be focused. Unfortunately, unless you are employed in social media management, Facebook, Twitter and Instagram will always find themselves in Quadrant 4.

I have included a time quadrant template for you to use (see appendices). Go ahead, knock yourself out! It always amuses me what ends up in Quadrant 4 ☺.

Taking Control

Taking control of one's life means being able to influence/ direct your own behavior and choices. In theory, it may seem easy, but realistically many of us do not have control over our lives. We abdicate authority to other people or events, and many times just the whims of fate.

"Taking control of one's life means being able to influence/ direct your own behavior and choices."

Conversely, in our zeal to try to control everything, some of us become overtaxed, frustrated, and in a constant state of anxiety.

The main key to taking control of our lives is understanding and accepting that there are some things that we can control, and others we cannot. If there are things out of our sphere of control, then belaboring over them is a waste of time. It logically then follows that concentrating on what you can control is a more efficient use of time.

For the purpose of this book, I want to focus on the controllables vs uncontrollables. Let us examine the uncontrollables. Some uncontrollables are:

• Other people	• Who's in your family
• Gas prices	• The past
• Traffic	• Death
• Weather	• Taxes
• Balding	• Natural disasters
• Economy	

Seems to be a long list, right? Let's look at some of the controllables:

• Effort exerted	• Thoughts
• Attitude	• Saying yes/no
• Level of honesty	• Speech
• Preparedness	• What you consume
• Response to situations	• Amount of exercise
• Response to situations	• Amount of sleep
• Time spent	

Wow! We have control over way more than we imagined! I read some-where once that what other people say or think about you is none of your business. Using that same logic, effort exerted over uncontrollables is wasted effort. If you can in no way affect change on a circumstance, why lose sleep over it? There are so many other things that you can control. My working theory is that focusing and mastering the controllables gives you the power to manage the uncontrollables.

Controllables vs.
UNCONTROLLABLES

UNCONTROLLABLES

- Other People
- Gas Prices
- Traffic
- Weather
- Balding
- Economy
- Who's In Your Family
- The Past
- Death
- Taxes
- Natural Disasters

CONTROLLABLES

CONQUERING THE CONTROLLABLES GIVES YOU
THE POWER TO ACCEPT/DEAL WITH/MANAGE
THE UNCONTROLLABLES

POWER

- Effort Exerted
- Attitude
- Level of Honesty
- Preparedness
- Response to Situations
- Thoughts
- Saying Yes/No
- Speech
- What You Consume
- Amount of Exercise
- Time Spent
- What You Learn
- Amount of Sleep

> *If you can in no way affect change on a circumstance, why lose sleep over it?*

So, let's practice. One major uncontrollable is other people. Contrary to what you may think or feel, you have no control over another person's thoughts or deeds. The controllable that you need to harness in this instance is your response to situations. You, and only you, are responsible for what you say and how you act. Take control and respond appropriately.

Let's do another one. How about the weather? Can any of us determine the time of sunrise or sunset? When and how often it rains or snows? Absolutely not! Then why complain? (It baffles me every year when I hear people complain about how cold it is in New York City in January and February. Guess what? It's winter, and winter in NYC is cold every year – but I digress.) If you can't affect the weather, the controllable to focus on is your preparedness. Check the weather for the next day. Will you need extra layers, rain boots or sunscreen? The goal is to focus on which controllable can be used to manage the uncontrollable you're faced with.

1. What are some things that have been frustrating you? Write them down.

_____

_____

_____

_____

_____

_____

_____

_____

_____

_____

_____

2. Divide the list under the headings of controllables and uncontrollables.

_____

_____

_____

_____

_____

_____

_____

_____

_____

_____

_____

_____

3. For each uncontrollable, choose which controllable you will master to mitigate against it.

_____

_____

_____

_____

_____

_____

_____

_____

_____

_____

Summary

Things to do after completing this section:

 • Create an exhaustive to-do list.

 • Complete the time quadrant template using the list.

 • Choose three controllables that you believe will have the most

 impact on your daily decisions, and commit to mastering them.

 Remember to add this task to your weekly goal sheet!

NOTES

SECTION 4

MASTERING
THE ART OF FAILURE

We are all failures . . . at least the best of us are.

– J.M. Barrie

WHAT TO EXPECT

- How to change your perspective about failure
- How to face your fears
- Learn how to use your failures to promote future success

The very title of this chapter makes you cringe. Who wants to master failing? It is said that the road to success is littered with failures. It makes the most sense that one should master it, thereby making navigating the path easier. In this book, we discuss success, so it would be negligent of me not to teach you how to deal with failure. But firstly, to confront the enemy, we must know the enemy. What is failure? Failure is defined as a lack of success. However most of us become preoccupied with the phrase "lack of", and view failure as personal indictment of us as persons. From a totally linguistic point of view, if failure is the lack of success, shouldn't the emphasis then be on defining success, and henceforth determining if we lack that quality? We are cognizant of the fact that our experiences of failure definitely color our outlook on life negatively and adversely affect our will to try again. But if by mere definition, failure is a close cousin of success, if we want to join the family, we must master the art of failing. So let's look at some simple steps.

CHANGE YOUR PERSPECTIVE

We have been socialized to believe that failure is indicative of either something being intrinsically wrong with us, or our quest is misguided. Nothing could be further from the truth. The biggest truth in this process is your willingness to try. The person who never tries cannot fail at anything. Therefore, with regard to personal characteristics, the only thing that failure is indicative of is that you tried. It is not a negative reflection of who you are as a person. Changing our perspective on failure is critical for us in finding our way to success. By shifting your perspective and seeing failure as a stepping stone to success, you won't allow episodes of failure to pummel you into the dust. Life can be viewed as a series of do-overs. It's a constant process of practice makes perfect. Failures are merely hurdles on the race to success, thus in order to cross the finish line, we must learn to surmount these hurdles.

What words or feelings come to mind when you think about failure?

_____

_____

_____

_____

_____

_____

_____

_____

_____

_____

_____

FACE YOUR FEARS

When you were younger, you feared the monster in the closet or under your bed, until you found out they didn't exist. Or you were scared of the dark, until you realized the dark wasn't that bad. Facing failure repeatedly not only makes failing less daunting, but also builds muscle. Facing failure means accepting that it happened. This is of course painful. However, being mired in your emotions is a waste of precious time and energy. S%^t happens, that's a part of life. Real success comes from cutting the pity party short, assessing the situation so that you can solve the problem. You get so good at this, failures don't faze you anymore. You are no longer knocked down, you roll with the punches and keep going.

What are you most afraid of failing at?

_____

_____

_____

_____

_____

_____

_____

_____

_____

_____

_____

_____

_____

LEARN FROM THE SCREW-UPS

Does failure mean the end or another route to success?

So, what, you didn't win this time? But what did you learn? Even with perfection, success is not guaranteed. Every keyboard has a backspace/delete key. Does failure mean the end or another route to success? Failure is synonymous with progress, the blueprint to success. We have heard numerous times that when Edison was asked about his many failures before making the light bulb, he said he learned the many ways not to make a light bulb. Focus on what you learned from the experience. Learn to make a change. Superstars don't let failure master them, they master it. They do this by accepting failure, objectively assessing their options, and taking constructive action.

What lesson did you learn from your last episode of failure?

_____

_____

_____

_____

_____

_____

_____

_____

_____

_____

IGNORE THE HATERS

This is, of course, the biggie. If we could only fail in privacy without other persons dwelling on and publicly discussing it, maybe we could survive. We need, however, to master the art of not reflecting personal feelings of shame. Allowing what other persons say about our failures to feed our own sense of insecurity and defeat is an absolute no-no. The truth is people will talk whether we fail or succeed, so practice ignoring them. If that seems hard, try even harder to succeed. There is no greater revenge than success.

Think of the greatest scandal to rock the country last year. Write it down.

_____

_____

_____

_____

_____

_____

_____

_____

_____

_____

One of two things happened to you while responding to the above scenario. One, either you couldn't pinpoint or remember one major scandal. Or two, nobody is talking about it anymore, so it has lost its importance. I come from the Caribbean where we call this a "nine-day wonder." No matter how juicy the story, it too will fade. The question for you is, will you allow the naysayers to cripple you and stifle your dreams?

Will you allow the naysayers to cripple you and stifle your dreams?

Defeated hopes offer you the opportunity to recalibrate – to reload, to re-think – why and how something didn't turn out as you'd anticipated. Feedback is often crucial to success, but you have to make an attempt to see the result and hear the feedback. Those who fear failure and rejection can "aim" indefinitely but never actually fire in their attempts to avoid further disappointment. Successful individuals – choosing to be pro-active rather than to procrastinate – are much readier to risk failure than forego what might be a valuable opportunity. When successful individuals miss their target, well, they just re-aim and take another shot – knowing that with each successive attempt, they're likely to get closer to the bullseye. Each miss is calculated not in terms of failure, but progress.

Regarding every failure, every rejection, as a learning opportunity is the best way to avoid letting setbacks deter you from continuing toward your goals. Ultimately, disappointments have only as much power as you choose to give them. Once you can "befriend" your failures and rejections, paradoxically, they can actually support your future efforts. If, however, you define failure and rejection self-defeatingly, they'll continue to control you. And they'll even doom you to further disappointments because of the resignation that comes with such a pessimistic attitude. If, on the other hand, you can see such defeats as an inevitable part of life, as something you must learn to deal with courageously and creatively, you're hardly likely to succumb to them. Future obstacles can almost always be reframed as challenges; and once you've effected this transformative mental shift, that last defeat will become your next opportunity. What felt like "the end" can now become a new beginning. And in affirming yourself in the face of failure and rejection, you will have truly mastered them.

The opposite of failure is success. Therefore, success is the other side of failure. So the great news is, if you have failed and want to succeed, all you have to do is turn over!

Summary

Things to do after completing this section:

- Document a previous failure. Please see appendices for a template you can use.
- Write down the lesson you learned from this failure.
- List the steps you are taking to correct the mistakes and try again.

NOTES

8 STEPS
TO SUCCESS

The distance between insanity and genius is measured only by success.

– Bruce Feirstein

WHAT TO EXPECT

- Learn how to define personal success
- Learn how to apply the eight steps to success

Success is defined as the accomplishment of an aim or purpose. Then it is logical to assume that if you don't have an aim or purpose, you cannot be successful. What is interesting, however, is that success is not defined as any one thing like money, wealth, power or recognition. It stands to reason, then, that you as an individual define your own success based on your plan for your life. Having come to that conclusion, let's outline eight simple steps to get you on the road to success.

"Success is defined as the accomplishment of an aim or purpose."

STEP
01
HAVE AN A ++++ ATTITUDE!

It is your attitude at the beginning of a difficult task which, more than anything else, will affect its success.

– William James

Your attitude affects your altitude. This is so because your attitude affects your outlook. Telling yourself you **can** is half the battle. The battle starts in the mind – make sure you win that round!

TIPS TO IMPROVING YOUR ATTITUDE

Always expect the best:
Expectations are self-controlled. We ultimately determine what we expect. Making a conscious effort to expect the best makes us predisposed to feel good, thus improving our attitude.

Wake up early:
Starting early creates the feeling of starting afresh. Starting a new day early can give us the feeling of taking control and dictating what happens. Having control of one's life is a good way to improve our attitude.

Exercise more:
 It is well documented that exercise has physical and psychological benefits for our bodies. By implementing some form of exercise – walking, running, gym or any other – we increase the chances of feeling better physically, and having a better attitude.

Surround yourself with positive persons:
We are a product of our environment. Subconsciously we absorb/adapt the behaviors of the persons we spend the most time with. If we know this to be a fact, then it makes sense to constantly be in the company of uplifting and positive persons.

Never compare yourself with others:
Whether we like it or not, there will always be persons who are better or worse than we are. Therefore, constantly comparing ourselves with others is an exercise in futility, as we're either going to be incredibly

vain or depressed. Concentrate on being your best you. If you know you've done your best, then that's all that matters.

Develop a habit of being grateful:
Being grateful forces us to focus on the positives in our life. When you constantly think about the good things that we have, we tend to be more appreciative and feel better about our circumstances.

STEP
02
BE ON TIME

If you're early, you're on time.
If you're on time, you're late.

– Lik Hock Yap Ivan

One of the oldest nursery rhymes teaches us that the early bird catches the worm. Being on time is an excellent habit to possess. Not only does it oftentimes make you able to seize opportunities that others can't, it also demonstrates professionalism and respect for others. Many decisions on whether or not to hire someone are based on their punctuality. Being punctual communicates that you are reliable and trustworthy. This can be a goal that you set in your weekly plan and work towards achieving.

STRATEGIES FOR BEING ON TIME

Plan your day the night before:
Having a plan allows for seamless execution. Taking the time to document activities overnight gives clarity of thought, opportunities to prioritize, and purpose of action.

Set an alarm:
Most of us need to be woken in the morning. Even if you are an early riser, setting an alarm provides the assurance that you will awake on time.

Get up the first time your alarm goes off:
We all have fallen victim to snuggling a few extra minutes. That leads to 10, then 15 minutes, and before you know it, we're scrambling around because we are so late. Fight the urge to snuggle under the covers – get up immediately.

Place the phone/clock out of reach:
Place your alarm far enough that you have to physically get out of bed to turn it off. If you have to get out of bed to turn it off, you will be less inclined to crawl back into bed.

Go to bed on time:
One of the main reasons we have a problem getting out of bed in the morning is because of lack of sleep. Getting to bed on time will ensure that you are properly rested to take on your day.

STEP
03
BE PREPARED

Opportunity doesn't make appointments, you have to be ready when it arrives.

– Tim Fargo

" If you are prepared to succeed you will always be lucky!"

It is said that luck is what occurs when preparation meets opportunity. If you are prepared to succeed you will always be lucky! Being prepared, however, is more than a mindset. It is putting into action plans to develop the skills and character to undertake the journey to success. Practical ways of doing this are making sure that your wardrobe has more than jeans, and that you're able to eat properly in a formal setting. Guess what? You would hate to be approached to attend a function at the White House and have nothing to wear and be unable to participate in a formal dinner setting!

HOW TO BECOME A PREPARER-IN-CHIEF

Understand the importance of being prepared:

Contrary to common belief, being prepared is not about being ready for disasters, it's about being ready for opportunities. When you fully understand and appreciate this concept, your perspective will totally shift from expecting the worst to being ready to capitalize on the best.

Have a plan:

The core of being prepared is having a plan. Designing a plan provides purpose and clarity. This in turn gives rise to examining as many outcomes or mishaps as possible. When a plan is in place, you are also better equipped to grasp opportunities, as the foundation for execution will already have been laid.

> *" The core of being prepared is having a plan."*

Be flexible:

Despite our best intentions, mishaps occur. Be flexible enough to be able to roll with the punches. Most importantly, it is the art of flexibility that will allow you to recognize those opportunities when they arise, and make things happen!

STEP
04
WORK YOUR PLAN

A good plan violently executed now is better than a perfect plan executed next week.

– George S. Patton

Some of us are excellent at documenting a plan, then shelving it. The plan must be executed. Do not allow fear of failure to cripple you. Get up and just do it!

What do you need to do to execute your plan?

THE BEST WAY TO EXECUTE A PLAN

Be focused:

Focus provides the clarity necessary to make decisions that support your most important goals. It results in a clearly-defined pathway to success. A sharp focus answers the "what" question:

What do you need to do to execute your plan?

How will you execute your plan?

Build your competence:

Competence is used here in the broadest sense of the term. It encompasses all the skills, systems, processes, and tools you use to achieve your goals. The result is the ability to commit to, measure and hit your targets. Building competence answers the "how" question: How will you execute your plan?

Why are you executing your plan?

Get excited:

Passion creates a sense of connectedness. It builds a connection between our human need for meaningful work and a sense of value and contribution. Igniting passion answers the "why" question: Why are you executing your plan?

STEP
05
WORK YOUR FULL 8 HOURS

*Commitment means staying loyal to what you said you were going do,
long after the mood you said it in has left you.*

– Anonymous

My use of 8 hours is just a figure that depicts a typical work day. The gist of it is that you keep going until the job gets down. Speak with any of your rap icons or movie stars, and they will tell you their days are long. You see the glitz and the glamour, but long hours go into making it happen. You cannot expect to achieve success by only investing minimal time. What you consistently practice is what you become.

" What you consistently practice is what you become. "

MASTERING THE ART OF STICK-TO-IVITY

Visualize the goal:
The journey is often long and arduous, but we must keep the end goal in mind. Keeping that visual constant will keep alive the will to continue long after the desire dies.

Commit to work now and play later:
The reality is that life is made up of work and play. If you choose to play in the first half, be prepared to work in the second half. Acknowledging

this reality and switching gears early will get you where you want to be.

Get an accountability partner:

As we discussed earlier, many of us need a third party to keep us on task, to essentially shame us into doing what we said we would do.

STEP
06

DON'T LOSE YOUR ATTITUDE

Excellence is not a skill, it is an attitude.

– Ralph Marston

By the time you start putting in your 8-hour days consistently, your positive attitude may begin to slip. Remember that the battle begins in the mind, so you cannot afford to lose your attitude. Know your warning signs and, when you feel the attitude declining, take a break to relax and recharge and look at how far you have come. Sometimes a simple change of pace or scenery will do the trick.

TIPS TO MAINTAINING YOUR ATTITUDE

Get enough sleep:

This cannot be over emphasized. Have you ever seen a toddler have a meltdown after missing a nap? While we may not have a tantrum, (I hope ☺), when we are tired we tend not to respond at our best, resulting in our attitudes going downhill.

Eat properly:

The Snickers effect is true, you're not you when you're hungry ☺. Have proper meals and healthy snacks when necessary to keep the sugar level up. Classmates, co-workers and family members are not edible. Eating when necessary will prevent you from trying to take a bite out of them.

Exercise:

It is not an urban legend, exercise is a natural feel good job! When I start my day with 30 minutes at the gym, I feel like I can take on the world! Try it, you will be pleasantly surprised.Take control of your thoughts and words: What you constantly think and say will become your reality. Avoid negative and pessimistic thoughts, and make a conscious effort to change the content and tone of your language. When someone asks how you're doing, avoid saying: "Could be better". Instead use phrases like "I'm fantastic!", or "I'm blessed!" Constant positive affirmations will seep into your attitude and translate into a positive outlook.

AVOID NEGATIVE PEOPLE:

This is a biggie. We all know persons that no matter what is happening, they **always** see the negative side of things. If it's raining, it's a bad day. If it's sunny, it's too hot. These kinds of persons can never be pleased or satisfied: Avoid them like the plague. The last thing you need when you're trying to hang on to your positive attitude is to be sucked into a "neg fest."

STEP
07
KNOW WHY YOU'RE HERE

In absence of clearly defined goals, we become strangely loyal to performing daily acts of trivia.

– Robert Heinlein

This is the importance of goal-setting. You must have a constant reminder of what you're working towards, so that when you become tired and discouraged you have something to cling to. I recommend getting a study card and writing on it your ultimate end goal and keeping it with you at all times. For example, My name is _____.

I am a _____ and I run my own company. I live at _____ and I drive a _____. Every year I vacation _____ and spend most of my free time_____.

DISCOVERING YOUR PERSONAL 'WHY', REMEMBERING WHAT'S AT STAKE

What makes you smile? There is something that warms everyone's heart. Pause and seriously think about what gives you that inner glow. That is the starting point of your "why."

If money and circumstances weren't an issue, what would you do? After the initial response of eating and sleeping all day ☺, what would you really do? This may take a while, because we are naturally inclined to make life decisions based on finances and familial pressure. Spend time on this point, it's really important.

Who is the single most important person in your life? Unfortunately, sometimes we can't persevere for ourselves, but we will do anything for that special someone. Who is that person in your life?

STEP
08
TAKE CONTROL

If you don't design your own life plan, chances are you'll fall into someone else's plan. And guess what they have planned for you? Not much.

– Jim Rohn

This is super important! Making a plan and executing it gives you control. You decide what you want to happen and then you make it happen. If you stay in the passenger seat of your life, you will never have control of what happens, as someone else holds the steering wheel.

HOW TO WREST CONTROL OF YOUR LIFE WITHOUT DERAILING IT

Define who you are and what you want: Being in control has a lot to do with being able to define who you are, what you want, and where you want to go. When you get the hang of this, the first hurdle is crossed. Review Section 1, if you're still wavering.

Perfect the art of saying 'no': The person who is in control of their life knows how to say no. You cannot be all things to everyone all the time – that is the recipe for handing over control to someone else. People will get their feelings hurt, but being in control means that you are first and foremost responsible for your feelings, not those of others.

Take pride in being different: Be proud of your uniqueness! Pride in your personal brand demonstrates confidence. A confident person is a person who is in control.

Remember to recharge: You're in control now, so remember the most important person – you! One of the greatest signs of someone in control of their life is the person who recognizes the importance of "me" time, and implements strategies to make it happen.

8
STEPS TO SUCCESS

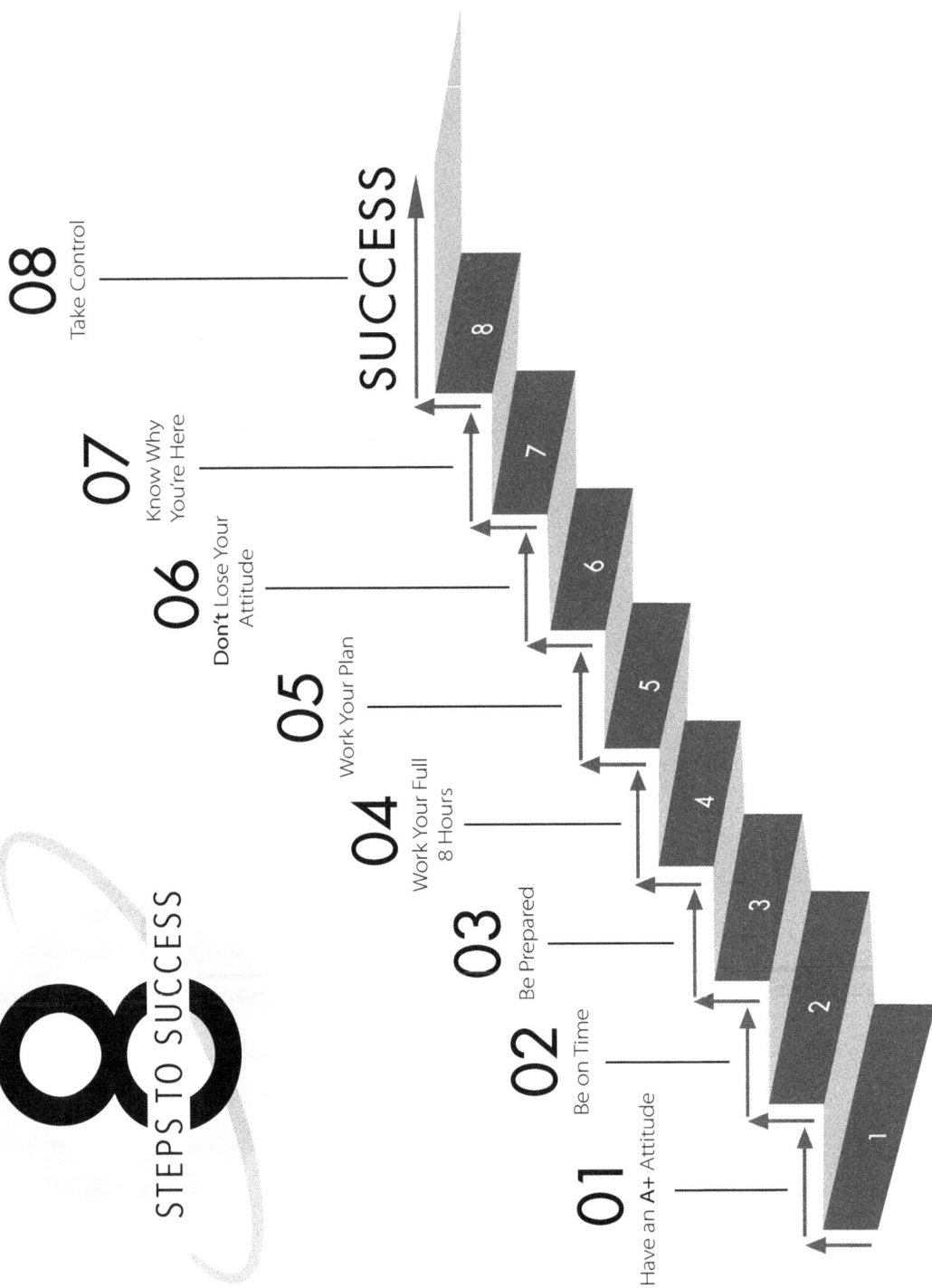

01 Have an A+ Attitude

02 Be on Time

03 Be Prepared

04 Work Your Full 8 Hours

05 Work Your Plan

06 Don't Lose Your Attitude

07 Know Why You're Here

08 Take Control

SUCCESS

Summary

Things to do after completing this section:

- Create a vision board. Use pictures and words of affirmation that support who you want to be and what you want to achieve. Remember to have fun!

NOTES

CONCLUSION

Making Me Happen is not just a project, it is the project. The greatest investment that you can make is in yourself. I know it is hard. Frankly, taking the decision to change is hard but it is well worth it. Working systematically through this book is a step in the right direction. ***Congratulations!*** Remember that you are **never** alone, our support group stands ready and willing to assist. Self-actualization is a continuous process, making improvements, constantly building on previous successes, and learning from past failures. Your ultimate goal is within reach. I believe in ***you***. I ***dare*** you to believe in ***YOURSELF!***

WORKSHEET
TEMPLATES

WEEKLY
G O A L S

WEEK OF: _____   NAME: _____

MY GOALS FOR THIS WEEK

1. _____
2. _____
3. _____

DAYS OF THE WEEK	RESULT GOALS	ACTION GOALS	ACHIEVED (Y/N)
M			
T			
W			
T			
F			
S			
S			

PERSONAL
SWOT ANALYSIS

INTERNAL FACTORS

STRENGTHS (+)

Talk about what you're good at, your unique assets and resources, and how your positive attributes are perceived by others.

WEAKNESSES (-)

Talk about improvements you need to make, any resources you lack, and how these negative attributes might be perceived by others.

S

W

EXTERNAL FACTORS

OPPORTUNITIES (+)

List doors that are currently open to you, opportunities you can capitalize on, and how your strengths can create new connections.

THREATS (-)

List any harmful hazards, competitors, and how known weaknesses can open the door to threats.

O

T

TIME QUADRANT

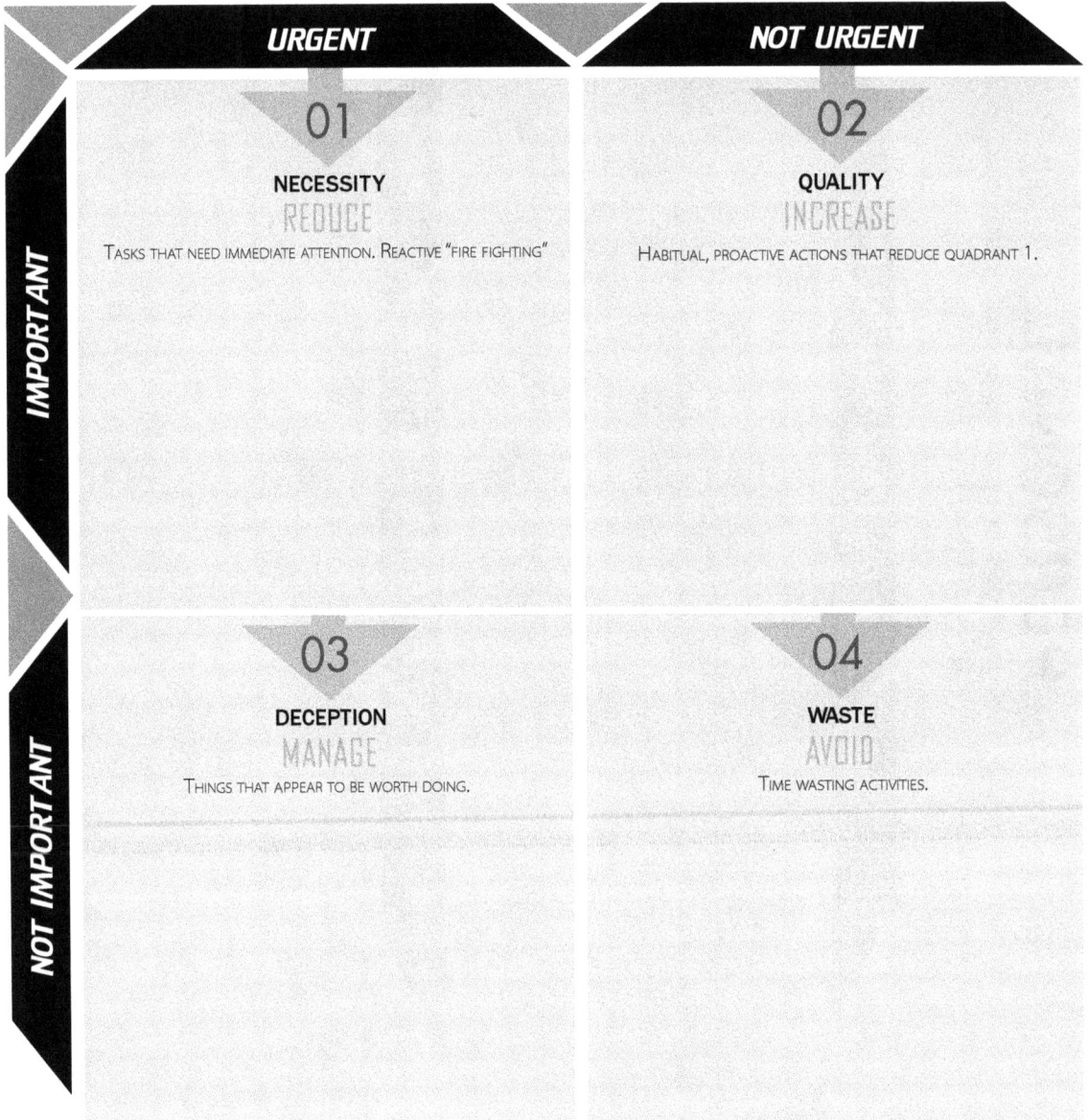

	URGENT	**NOT URGENT**
IMPORTANT	**01** **NECESSITY** REDUCE Tasks that need immediate attention. Reactive "fire fighting"	**02** **QUALITY** INCREASE Habitual, proactive actions that reduce quadrant 1.
NOT IMPORTANT	**03** **DECEPTION** MANAGE Things that appear to be worth doing.	**04** **WASTE** AVOID Time wasting activities.

FIXING MY FAILURES

01 LIST SOME INSTANCES OF TIMES YOU FAILED

02 WHAT DID YOU LEARN FROM YOUR FAILURES

03 LIST YOUR WHY'S: *THE THINGS THAT KEPT YOU MOVING FORWARD*

SUGGESTED
READING

The 7 Habits of Highly Effective Teens
by Sean Covey

The 6 Most Important Decisions You'll Ever Make
by Sean Covey

Chicken Soup for the Teenage Soul on Tough Stuff:
Stories of Tough Times and Lessons Learned
by Jack Canfield, Mark Victor Hansen, and Kimberly Kirkberger

The Secret to Teen Power
by Paul Harrington

The Shyness and Social Anxiety Workbook for Teens:
CBT and ACT Skills to Help Build Social Confidence
by Jennifer Shannon and Doug Shannon

NOTES

MAKING ME
HAPPEN

www.ingramcontent.com/pod-product-compliance
Lightning Source LLC
Chambersburg PA
CBHW062046090426
42740CB00016B/3041